A Miracle of Love

A Miracle of Love

by

Frances B. Lancaster

Dear Kyle —
Love
Grandma L.

A Miracle of Love

©2013, Frances B. Lancaster

WiseWoman Press

Vancouver, WA

www.wisewomanpress.com

ISBN: 978-0-945385-86-8

Printed in the USA

Dedication

To our children, Brent and Katrina
for their loving and faithful support
through a most difficult time
of transition for my husband
and their father

Table of Contents

Brent and Mom

A Time of Passing

Written December 21, 2012
The end of the Mayan Calendar

It must have been one of the saddest days of his life. My 40-year old son, Brent, was about to return home alone, a thousand miles away, and would never see or hear the voice of his father again. No more phone calls, advice for his projects, support for his accomplishments, encouragement in his challenges, nor physical assistance in his endeavors. Instead of withdrawing into his own sense of loss, Brent created miracles of love for his mother.

Brent missing his dad

John helping Brent

It's said that we get into relationships because we need someone to witness our lives, to acknowledge we exist. What Brent did touched my heart then and still touches my heart today, almost two years later.

50 Year Anniversary
Frances and John

Most of the physical gifts Brent left still hang where he left them; I'll explain that later on. I was touched deeply because he had become an attentive observer of his mother's life, her habits and daily activities. Truly, he was a witness to my life. His thoughtfulness contributed greatly to my healing process as I moved forward into a new phase of living after saying good-bye to my devoted husband of 53 years.

I waited patiently in the car for Brent to come out of the house and join me the last day of his visit after John's passing. We were on our way to the airport so he could catch his flight back to his home in southern California.

Brent at work

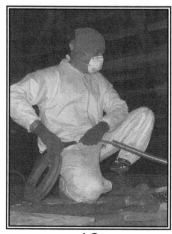

I had called before six AM that fateful morning when his dad became so sick. The hospice nurse insisted that I get help and contact my children.

It had been the worst night of my life and no doubt the most terrifying of John's as well. Looking back, I can see that it was God's way of saying, "You can't do this alone anymore."

My son made arrangements to close down his business right away. Ironically, his wife and her 80-year old aunt had made plans to visit relatives in another country, so he came alone.

Katrina and John

For six days, Brent, his sister Katrina, and I kept watch over John. The purple splendor azaleas were in full bloom and could be seen through the sliding patio doors. We kept a fire burning in the wood stove.

Katrina

Katrina with her husband, Clarence

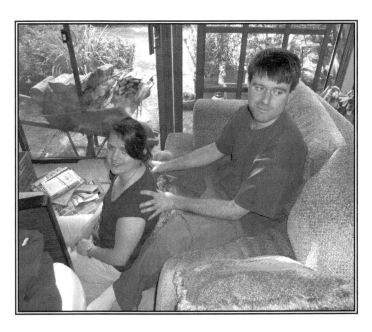

Katrina with her brother Brent

Katrina was just beginning her Hospice train-
ing as part of her re-entry program into
nursing. It was her mentor's company that
was chosen for Hospice which turned out to
be a miracle in itself.

John was so happy when both she and Brent and I were with him. It was a very special time of giving and receiving love and nurturing. It is a great privilege to shepherd a loved one into the next dimension. We were blessed to have had this opportunity to be fully present, just the three of us for most of the time.

Hospice had sent out a special bed which was placed in the living room, and when John saw the bed, he was really pleased.

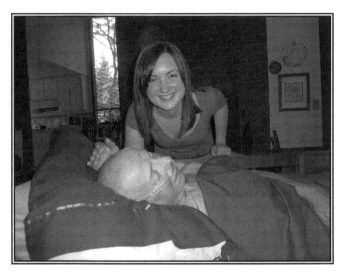

Granddaughter Melody
Comforting Grandpa

At first he was able to converse with us, and a few neighbors, friends and relatives came by to pay their respects. The grandchildren came and were able to share their gratitude for his unfailing love and devotion.

He was never alone those six days. In the evening, one of us slept beside him on the sofa in case he needed anything. He could see the fire in the fireplace, which he loved, hear the soft music, and enjoy the lovely garden setting during daylight hours.

He passed quietly around eight PM on May 17, 2011, just after his son-in-law had left. We held him, prayed and blessed him when his last breath was taken. Each of us experienced our deepest feelings at our loss and tried to comfort each other the best that we could.

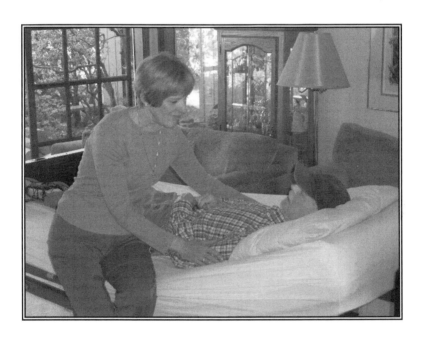

We picked out his favorite outfit, a pair of jeans and a plaid cotton shirt and the baseball hat he was never without. We dressed him and let him rest for the remainder of the evening in his bed.

Katrina stayed on the couch beside him. In the morning people from the mortuary came and respectfully removed him from our home as our hearts sank with the realization we would never see him again.

Remembering

It was Brent who took charge of a slide show for the memorial service. He wanted to present the many sides of his beloved father and couldn't bear to make the event a somber occasion. He scanned dozens of photos, divided them into various categories, mixed in a little humor and played country western music behind the presentation.

Family Man

Humorist
Woodsman
Sailor

Friends helped arrange the bouquets of flowers that adorned the church, most of which
came directly from our garden; in the spring
our yard is like a giant flower basket. Other
momentous were presented for people to enjoy.

One was a picture of John holding a praying mantis. He loved nature, taught science and at one time had a huge collection of insects that were mounted in a display case.

I'm a minister and planned the remaining part of the service, although a good friend and minister of Unity officiated at the ceremony.

I was able to begin with the story about an eagle that was raised with chickens and had to be taught to fly. John was like the eagle, raised in an environment that he chose to soar high above in his lifetime through determination and hard work.

Zach, Clarence, Melody, Kyle, John, Katrina

Katrina and our grandchildren, Zachary, Melody and Kyle had all written something to read at the service. People were amazed by how our grandchildren had conducted themselves.

A dear friend played several of his favorite songs to a packed church.

The one comment we heard many times was, "That was the best memorial service I've ever attended."

It was extremely satisfying to know that we had given John such an honorable sendoff.

He was truly a family man and did everything he could to be a good provider and make life interesting, comfortable, and fun.

Brent's Miracles

Getting back to our trip to the airport, Brent took an extra long time coming out to the car. I didn't think much about it at the time, but when I got home I discovered what the delay had been.

Here's where the miracles began again. After 53 years of marriage, one might expect a terrible sense of loss and depression for the widow. Brent was anticipating this difficulty and decided he could do something to ease the pain.

Inside refrigerator

One of the first things I did when I got back from the airport was to open the refrigerator. There I found a little strip of paper about 2 inches long and half an inch wide stuck to the shelf.

That was to be the first of many white papers with type-written messages placed in strategic locations all over my home.

You may be wondering what the messages said. Brent understands his mother's daily activities and followed his heart to inspire love in all the important places.

The strip of paper in the refrigerator said, "I love you."

Immediately my heart warmed when I realized he had been thinking ahead and wanted me to know I was thought of and wasn't really alone.

Cup of Water?....

Most recent display of
forgotten cups!

That would have been enough and I was grateful for his effort, but when I went to open the microwave, there was a cup of water with another strip of paper.

It said, "Cup of water?..."

It has been a habit of mine to put a cup of water in the microwave, turn on the one minute button, walk away, and never come back till hours later to retrieve the" by then" cold water!

He knew this and figured I would get a laugh when seeing the message. I did laugh for sure. I haven't changed my habit, though, so I've left the wrinkled little paper attached to the top of the microwave all these months.

My next surprise came when I opened the silverware drawer. I guess my son knew some elderly people or at least conjured that living alone, I might take a few short cuts when it came to meal time.

He was right, but more than once I've made sure that I put down a placemat on the counter and set the table in a decent way before eating. The note in the silverware drawer said, "You're worth setting the table for."

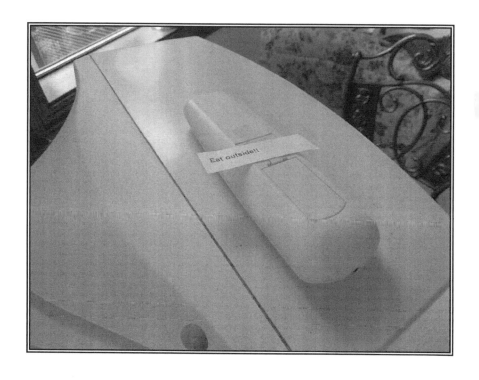

It was late spring when John passed on. It had been our tradition to eat outside whenever the weather permitted it. We have a gazebo in the garden and it's a delightful place to sit among flowers, watch the birds and butterflies and just enjoy the peace of our beautiful yard.

Brent was well aware of this past time. I picked up the remote for the TV that was on the kitchen counter where I was about to eat. To my amazement, there was a note attached to the underside. You guessed it! The note said, "Eat outside."

Brent thinking of things to write
on those strips of paper.

My goodness! He was quite a busy person while I waited in the car for him that day long ago. I know my son is one of a kind, and I feel really blessed to be so well looked after. But how many people would take the trouble to type out those little strips of paper or even think of the activities in which a recent widow might need encouragement? He certainly had no precedent for this kind of action in neither our family, nor anyone I knew of.

Wind The Clock!

60

I walked into the front hallway and noticed something hanging from the grandfather clock. It's the kind of clock that rings on the quarter hour throughout its cycle. My husband loved clocks and acquired quite an assortment of them which our children have now sorted out as their future possessions when the time comes to divvy them up.

The white strip of paper partially blocking the face of the clock said, "Wind the clock." I've been pretty good about that, thanks to his note. I've only had to restart it about 3 times in all these months.

Since then, sometimes the chimes hang down pretty close to the bottom of the case, but I hear a voice whispering, "Wind the clock." Is that Brent's voice? Or John's?

The front door is to the right of the clock. I haven't touched that note. It shows off against the dark wood and is a good reminder of the job I am supposed to do, especially before going to bed or leaving the house for the day. It simply says, "Lock the front door."

Later that first day after Brent left, I wandered into the study where we created a space for our cat including his litter box. Spike had become very attached to John, and at times it seemed that he could tell when John wasn't doing very well. When shut up in the room at night, he would sometimes howl, reflecting the restlessness that John was experiencing with his heart condition.

It is uncanny, but animals can be very sensitive to their owner's difficulties, especially health issues. He knew something was wrong, but what could a cat do? This cat was very vocal, however, and tried to take over whenever possible.

It was laughable when I walked into the den that afternoon and found a strip of paper hanging from the doorway of the covered litter box. Brent was reminding me, "Spike is not in charge!" Within the year Spike had gone on to be with John.

Actually, a couple of psychic friends told me that they had "seen" John in the Vet's office when Spike was given the injection to relieve him of his incurable disease. It was a very sad time for me as Spike had been a comfort to me, a reminder of John's devotion and love.

I thought I hadn't taken a picture of that note, but a week ago I climbed up in the attic to get January decorations down. I looked over my shoulder and there to my surprise was the litter box, stuffed with the cat's bed.

The note was still hanging from the lid where Brent had placed it.

I found two other little greetings placed where I would be sure to find them. One was on the shower door in the master bedroom, and another was attached to the inside of our walk-in closet.

Both said, "I love you." Well, they still say, "I love you" and I don't plan on removing them any time soon.

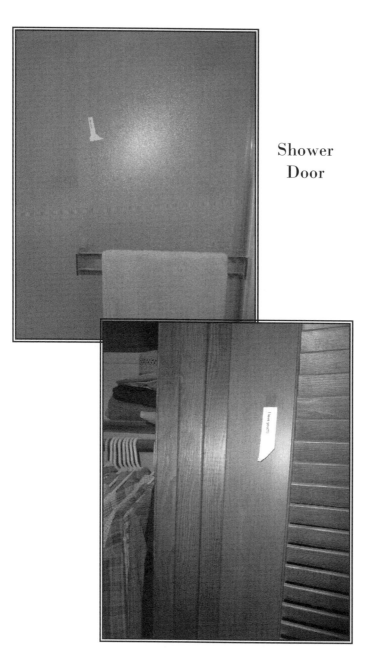

Shower
Door

Inside Bedroom Closet

69

I thought I had written about all the notes I found, but when I started looking through my photos, I found three more!

My son really knows his mother. He's apt to inform me that there is a left over hair from my blush brush lingering on my cheek. The note I found on my hairbrush reminded me to, "Use your glasses (makeup)"

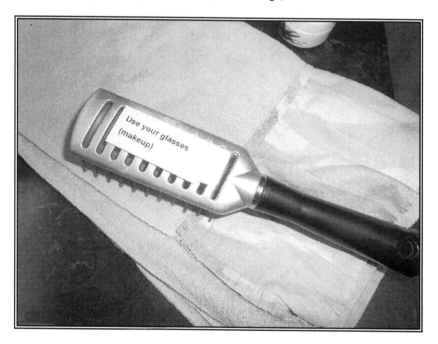

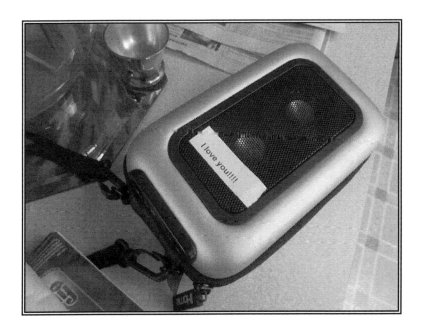

The second picture I found after I thought I was finished is a note that Brent put on my Mp3 speaker we bought at a garage sale. I teach classes and thought it would be easier to play music through this device rather than a boom box.

The note says, "I love you!!!!!"

This is another reason I feel so blessed. Every older adult needs someone who is savvy with electronic equipment. Our son got so tired of trying to figure out what "won't go" (my favorite trouble-call), that he built us a computer and arranged for us to be on line together. Life has been much easier for him since then.

Printer

Almost a year and a half later, while he was here on vacation fixing my non-working printer, Brent discovered one more of the messages he'd left for me!

It also says, "I love you!!!"

Final note.

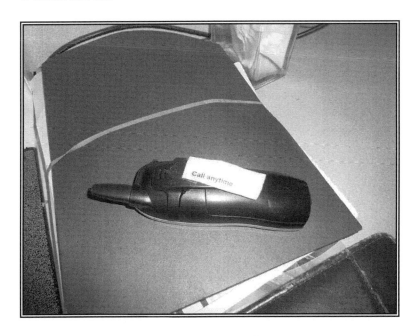

Can you guess what it says?

(Call anytime)

What a Difference!

I'm writing this story because we all face the possibility of losing a loved one, or know someone who is dealing with a loss. We may feel helpless in dealing with our own emotions at times or may feel helpless to support another move through their grieving process.

I've never heard of anyone doing what my son did in the way he did it, but his kindness and thoughtfulness were major influences in my recovery.

Camping was a favorite
pastime, still is!

His little notes reminded me that life goes on and that some of the things my husband and I shared could still be experienced although on a different level. There was a Spirit in me that seemed to fill me with love and appreciation more than the emptiness of loss.

John's presence is everywhere in our home. His creativity was boundless and his love for me and our children created a nest of safety and peace as we have all moved forward through our time of transitioning through his physical absence.

John's Carvings

John's
Collection
Of Fishing
Lures

What probably affected me most about the notes Brent left, was the fact that he anticipated my actions so accurately. He knew how I spent my time, what was important, what little things I'd be doing, and what ordinary things might slip onto the back burner without a little encouragement.

Mom creating things with Katrina

Mom having a good time with friends

THE KISS OF THE SUN
FOR PARDON.
THE SONG OF THE BIRDS
FOR MIRTH.
ONE IS NEARER GODS
HEART IN A GARDEN,
THAN ANY WHERE ELSE
ON EARTH.

Mom tending the garden and
spending time outdoors.

Brent's a modest person and wouldn't want any of this recognition, but his love is expressed so powerfully, that I hope this story will inspire others to really pay attention to those closest to them.

Our lives get rather self centered with computers, cell phones, game pads, work, and household chores. It takes effort to be fully present for any length of time, to know in detail some of our family members' greatest joys, heart aches, struggles, likes, and dislikes. Reaching across the age differences is even harder, especially when distance is a consideration.

Making Beautiful Memories

John and grandson Kyle
making a beautiful memory
Nature Center Eagle's nest

One of my favorite quotes is, "Live in the present and make it so beautiful that it will be worth remembering." I discovered it one day among house plants on my hearth. I don't know where it came from, but the words were recorded on a 4 inch tile.

Wouldn't it be wonderful if we could stop every once in awhile and ask, "How can I make a beautiful moment for someone?" There is a voice within us that always has bright ideas that bring good into our lives or into the life of someone else if we choose. When we find ourselves thinking about the well being of another person, something clicks inside of our hearts.

The very thought makes us feel good, and when we combine that thought with action, we start a chain reaction. It's like tossing a pebble into a still pond. The ripples spread out much farther than the original splash.

Frances enjoying a beautiful moment.

Like a waterfall, generosity touches hearts and sends cascades of goodness to places we never dreamed of.

There's a premise that says what we give comes back to us good measure, pressed down and multiplied. I think it comes back in the form that is most useful or heart-fulfilling to us.

Frances with her mother, Ruth,
celebrating a birthday together.

I had a great example in my mother. She was a giver into her 90's. She always looked for something to give me before I left her home even after a short visit. It might have been food she had cooked or an article she had cut from the newspaper that she thought either my husband or I would enjoy reading.

I remember when I was growing up that my mother would bake and give away plates of cookies at Christmas time. She and my dad loved flowers, and my mom would pick a bouquet of beautiful roses if we were going to visit a friend. I am grateful for her mentoring in this respect.

LIVE IN THE
PRESENT
AND MAKE IT SO
Beautiful
IT WILL BE WORTH
REMEMBERING.

In the past I have been a giver, but this time when it mattered most, I was on the receiving end. Perhaps the seeds I had "sown" elsewhere had taken root in my "garden."

Brent and Frances
Overlooking Mt. St. Helens

Paying It Forward

What Brent did made such a difference in my life. With every note, my heart opened with a new perspective. I mattered!

The things I valued were noticed, and I was reminded of the comfort and joy of the daily activities I would now be engaging in by myself.

Those little notes that said, "I love you" were reminders that I wasn't alone in transitioning to this new phase of life.

The Dalai Lama says his religion is "Kindness." Certainly this was a deep and sincere act of kindness. Its results were somewhat miraculous in how my life was blessed day by day upon seeing each of the various messages. Most of them still remain where he placed them!

Thoughtfulness inspires the spiritual gift of kindness. It requires a willingness to put ones self in another's "shoes." To do this, we must become "present." We must learn to connect at a deeper level with each other through observation and listening with our hearts.

Through acts of kindness we fulfill our higher purpose for being here on earth. We are reflecting the great love that brought us into this dimension in the first place.

Consider the power of intention. Until we harness the energy of possibility, magic moments slip away and a miracle is lost.

We might ask, "What would I like if I were facing that situation? There is a softer voice deep within us that is always ready to give us a higher thought, one that brings a feeling of love and peace.

As we make a habit of listening to this voice and practice acting on it, we are actually giving a great gift to ourselves as well.

When people are experiencing especially difficult situations, our gift of thoughtfulness can create a miracle. Our word or action can restore peace, bringing relief from a state of despair and emotional pain.

YOU and I can make a moment so beautiful that it will be worth remembering for ourselves and for another human being. We are demonstrating the most valued gift of all, Love.

The universe has within it a mechanism that returns what we give out. At a time in our own lives when we are facing a challenge, what we have "paid forward" in our good deeds, returns to us in a form that is helpful to us. This is how love works!

One day at a time we can begin anew to look for ways to be a beneficial presence. As we do, we will begin to surprise ourselves with the unexpected joy that bubbles up from within as we choose kindness. Our thoughtfulness becomes a habit, and life becomes extraordinary. We become angels, messengers of love.

May you be inspired to make a lasting difference wherever you go by listening to that soft
voice of love and following its guidance.

May you also be blessed in your time of need
by the thoughtfulness of a loved one, just as I
was blessed by my son, Brent.

Another tile that inspires me.

Thank you, Brent.

Your messages kept me present and helped to heal my heart.

I love you,

Mom

Completed May 17, 2013, two years after John's passing.

❤

About the Author

Rev. Frances Lancaster lives in Hillsboro, Oregon. She is an independent minister lecturing, teaching, writing and facilitating study groups. She has a degree in Education from Washington State University and has written curriculum for both adults and children in the Metaphysical movement. She has served in the leadership capacity of both local and international spiritual organizations. Her passion centers on helping people learn to create fulfilling and productive lives as they serve one another through conscious connection with our Creator's inspiration and guidance.

WISEWOMAN PRESS

Books Published by WiseWoman Press

By Frances B. Lancaster

- *Abundance Now*
- *13th Commandment*
- *Happiness Now*

By Emma Curtis Hopkins

- *Resume*
- *The Gospel Series*
- *Class Lessons of 1888*
- *Self Treatments including Radiant I Am*
- *High Mysticism*
- *Genesis Series 1894*
- *Esoteric Philosophy in Spiritual Science*
- *Drops of Gold Journal*
- *Judgment Series in Spiritual Science*
- *Bible Interpretations: Series I, thru XVII*

By Ruth L. Miller

- *Unveiling Your Hidden Power: Emma Curtis Hopkins' Metaphysics for the 21st Century*
- *Coming into Freedom: Emily Cady's Lessons in Truth for the 21st Century*
- *150 Years of Healing: The Founders and Science of New Thought*
- *Power Beyond Magic: Ernest Holmes Biography*
- *Power to Heal: Emma Curtis Hopkins Biography*
- *The Power of Unity: Charles Fillmore Biography*
- *Power of Thought: Phineas P. Quimby Biography*
- *The Power of Insight: Thomas Troward Biography*
- *The Power of the Self. Ralph Waldo Emerson Biography*
- *Gracie's Adventures with God (Editor)*
- *Uncommon Prayer*
- *Spiritual Success*
- *Finding the Path*

www.wisewomanpress.com